TACKLING SOCIAL ANXIETY IN THE SOCIETY

What you need to know

Table of contents

Aim of this book

Social phobia is a condition that affects about 7% of the population. This condition can be challenging and difficult to deal with, as it can completely deny a person the chance to reach their full potential in life. However, there are several ways to overcome social phobia.

In order to conquer social phobia and prevent anxiety from taking over your life, you should always try to do exactly the things that you are always afraid of or anxious about. Just like fear of heights, which can be tackled by exposing yourself to frightening situations, social phobia can also be dealt with by confronting social situations that you are always afraid of. This approach of tackling fear is known as *the common-sense formula* in many social phobia books. Combining this 'common sense' strategy with scientific suggestions and behavior therapy can help a lot in dealing with social phobia. The most effective social phobia treatment that has been found to work effectively is physiotherapy. This book discusses everything about social phobia and outlines various self-help tips that anyone struggling with this condition can follow in order to conquer the condition.

After reading this book, you'll have an in-depth understanding of the importance of changing the thoughts that normally lead to anxiety. To get a firmer grip on your condition, this book acts as a guide helping you to prepare well as you plan to deal with social phobia and how to deal with relapse.

The aim of this book is to help the reader conquer social phobia and come up with a solid plan for prevention of a relapse. After reading this book, it's important to talk to your therapist in order for them to help find and assess your progress. Your therapist will also answer some of your questions and provide further help necessary in the treatment of social phobia.

This book is ideal for anyone willing to embrace change after struggling with social phobia. This book helps you understand that social phobia can be overcome by following every strategy that has been discussed. The self-help strategies discussed in this book will help anyone serious about tackling social phobia and living a good life. If you are struggling with social phobia, all you have to do is to admit and embark on how to stop it. As an individual, you have a part to play if at all you want to defeat social phobia and get your social life back.

This book has everything covered from the definition of social phobia through symptoms to understanding the condition and different strategies that can be used in order to stop feeling anxious when talking to people or making new friends. This book comes with a DIY touch for anyone looking to overcome social phobia and prevent relapse. It will also act as a guide for anyone planning to replace negative way of thinking with a positive view of things in life.

This book has been compiled in order to help 7% (this figure was reached at courtesy of different studies carried out by various research bodies) of the population that is struggling with this condition around the world. Social phobia can lead to serious consequences in a person's life.

According to some studies conducted to uncover social phobia in the society, it was found that people who suffer from this condition are likely to feel lonely and indulge in drugs and alcohol in an effort to deal with fear and anxiety. Such individuals are also less likely to get a spouse or make new friends. People struggling with social phobia find it challenging maintaining relationships and friendships.

In summary, this book is designed to help you understand what social phobia means, its causes, general information on symptoms, self-help strategies, and how to identify and prevent relapse. The book also covers different treatment options for social phobia.

Introduction

It's absolutely right to say that the only thing to fear is fear itself. In a society that is rapidly changing and experiencing technological advancements on a regular basis, human beings are scared of what could be in store for them than ever before. Look at things like Artificial Intelligence, robots, and automation of processes that were once executed by human beings; technology is slowly taking over, and soon, we'll be seeing workers and professionals in certain fields becoming jobless. For instance, let's look at what the future holds for web developers out there after significant advancements in automated web development. It looks like professionals in many fields will become jobless in future, as the adoption of Artificial Intelligence looks inevitable.

Apart from fear caused by technological advancements, human beings are also scared of several other situations and events in life—one of them being terrorism. In a world where terrorism has become the order of the day, it looks like we are living in the most unsecure era ever. So many things happen in life. Some of them scare us, and some of them don't.

Some of the things we go through in this technology-mad society are actually the reason why we develop anxiety. We depend on technology but still fear it. We all have different fears in life. In some cases, we fear situations that we're still dependent on but have no control over. Some people fear being judged by others due to their actions while others fear certain things such as talking to a group of strangers or public speaking. We all encounter anxiety at some stage in life. The fear caused by a situation you don't believe in. To some people, this fear becomes an obstacle that never allows them to achieve healthy living and quality life. If not treated early enough, anxiety can rip apart a person's life and prevent them from achieving goals. However, if anxiety is the order of your daily life, several proven treatment strategies can help you enjoy life and conquer the fear.

Some of us sometimes encounter fear when speaking to an audience or when meeting new people. This fear manifests itself in different ways, making it hard to do certain things in public— participating in group discussions, making new friends, taking part in interviews, and socializing.

Meeting and talking to an audience for the first time sometimes makes a person feel shy and nervous. This is normal, especially if you've never done something close to that. Anxiety and fear is part of life. However, if this fear gets to a level where it rips your life apart by feeling nervous and fearing certain situations that would make you feel embarrassed or fear that others may judge and evaluate you in a negative way, that's not normal. It's a disorder or, let's just say, social phobia. If you often get nervous and anxious because you think that you might end up embarrassing and humiliating yourself doing something in public, then you may have social phobia. This disorder makes a person to feel that others may end up judging them by their actions or after maybe talking to an audience or a group of people, eating in public, using utilities like toilets, participating in small talk, starting conversations, talking to leaders, working, going to school or work, and public performances.

Worrying about these situations is sometimes common, but individuals who have social phobia become excessively nervous about them. This excessive nervousness is the problem. Almost everyone fears something, but this fear should not be chronic. This anxiety should not prevent us from achieving certain things in life. You'll realize that your fear of something has turned into social phobia the moment it starts preventing you from enjoying life by creating negative thoughts and guesses about social situations. By the end of this book, the reader will be able to manage social phobia and prevent relapse.

CHAPTER 1

Social Phobia Defined

Social phobia is a condition which makes a person feel nervous in social situations because they think that they are doing something wrong and people may end up humiliating and judging them in different ways. They experience sweating, stomach problems, shaking, increased breathing rate, and several other symptoms when speaking or meeting people. This condition can sometimes worsen to a degree where a person ends up not enjoying being around people or doing certain things such as eating or drinking.

People struggling with social phobia always fear all forms of social interaction forums. These people not only fear humiliation and embarrassment but also being evaluated negatively. Inferiority takes over them, coupled with anxiety, making it difficult attending parties or social functions. This severe anxiety and fear of social situations is known as social phobia. It affects a certain percentage of the population, making it difficult to talk or give a speech in front of an audience. We shall look at the symptoms and causes of social phobia later in this book.

When you start fearing that people will judge you out of your actions, then you are probably going through a condition known as social phobia. This condition often leaves a person worried about any situation that triggers fear symptoms. It sometimes makes a person to completely avoid anything that can expose them to fear. A majority of people with social phobia usually find it hard making new friends and maintaining relationships. In most cases, people who have social phobia prefer spending time with family members or close relatives rather than interacting with friends, workmates, or schoolmates. If staying close to family members doesn't make them avoid embarrassing situations, some will use drugs or alcohol to avoid being nervous.

This fear is usually very strong, sometimes forcing a person to avoid any situation they believe would embarrass or humiliate them. It normally starts when a person thinks that they will do something that will make them look stupid, incompetent, shy, weak, or just anxious. A person suffering from this condition may start shying away or sweating at a slight mention of a situation that, according to them, might make others start making conclusions about them.

Let's look at an example here: Jason graduated a few months ago with a computer science degree and landed a lucrative job as a system administrator at a tech firm. During one of the company's team-building sessions, the CEO asks Jason to make a presentation, but Jason suddenly starts sweating and becomes nervous. He tries all means possible to convince the CEO not to have him do the presentation. Meanwhile, he looks anxious and confused about the whole idea of making a presentation in front of workmates. Anxiety symptoms such as sweating, trembling, increased heart rate, and increased breathing rate begin to show up. He ends ups presenting his resignation letter immediately to avoid any situation that would make others to judge him. Jason has social phobia. Just like some people suffering from the same condition, Jason went ahead to avoid this situation altogether because he feared being judged, humiliated, and embarrassed.

In most cases, people who have social phobia in society fear speaking in public. Public speaking fear is something common. There are actually some celebrities that struggled with stage fright if you never knew. Performance anxiety, stuttering, and stage fright affected big names such as Tiger Woods, Bruce Willis, Samuel L. Jackson, and Vladimir Horowitz. Vladimir was a very famous performer and talented pianist who decided to retire early because of stage fright. He decided to make a comeback after this, but things still didn't work out.

Fear of public speaking affects people in different ways. There are different types of social phobia, as we shall see later.

Social phobia also makes a person start feeling anxious when in the company of others because it triggers worries that they may end up doing something stupid and embarrassing when contributing in a discussion or starting a small talk. The fear of being judged, coupled with anxiety and panic attacks, can be so bad to the extent of not being able to enjoy spending time with people maybe at your place of work or school.

There are some recommended ways to deal with social phobia, but the best treatment will always be learning how to control the fear as a person, accept the condition—even if it makes you feel that you are being judged. Even if it makes you look confused and shaken when talking to people, just ignore that thought and give yourself confidence. After all, they will only think that something must have been wrong with your day or maybe you were not at your best at that specific time. Later in this book, we shall cover the different strategies that can be used to confront social phobia.

The fear of certain situations in life normally leads to nervousness, which may sometimes drive a person to avoid particular situations that involve talking to a group of people or just contributing during meetings days before it happens.

This condition can worsen from an early age into adulthood if not treated early enough. Social phobia is not a new disorder. There are many people out there struggling with it on a daily basis. For instance, according to studies, about 7% of Americans have, at some stage in life, struggled with social phobia. If not treated early enough using the right treatment option, this condition can interfere with the quality of life of a person and prevent them from attaining the highest level in their daily activities.

It' important to comprehend that social phobia can become a problem to an extent where it becomes an obstacle in your life, making it hard to achieve the quality life you deserve. If you are suffering from this condition, you'll find that it can sometimes prevent you from making new friends or socializing in life. However, despite what social anxiety can make you go through, the good news is that there are different forms of treatment options that can help tackle the fears.

If you feel that social phobia has denied you the chance to achieve certain things in life, it's time to start thinking how to stop it. If you always fear that people will laugh at you because of mistakes you make, it's time to understand that not everyone is perfect, and you are not the only one struggling with this condition. Do not expect that everyone will like everything about you, including what you do. Ask yourself this question: Do I like everyone out there?

Start looking at your fears from a different perspective. Not everyone will notice that you are feeling nervous when talking to them. Furthermore, you are not the first or last person to struggle with social phobia. No matter what the people will think of you, being anxious is always part of life, and the good thing is that it can be treated. Instead of struggling with the fight within you and always fearing that people will judge you, why not concentrate on how to take back your life?

After looking at your situation from a different angle, you'll possibly find out that the things that you've always feared don't actually exist. If at all the anxiety happens to be real, then you'll realize that it's not as serious as you've always thought.

Is social phobia different from normal anxiety?

We sometimes describe ourselves as being shy without understanding what this actually means. Do we have the clear definition of what we mean when we describe ourselves as being shy? Normally, shyness occurs at different stages in life. It happens in childhood all the way until we become teenagers. Nervousness is a widespread occurrence among teenagers. However, as a person gets to adulthood, this shyness decreases with time.

In some cases, many people, including adults, find themselves struggling with this shyness, which develops into fear of certain social situations. Some adults still find it difficult to speak in public or interact freely with strangers not because they do not want to know them but because of fear of being judged negatively.

Such individuals normally start worrying about an upcoming event weeks or days early because of social phobia. They then find themselves panicking and confused while thinking about the humiliation or embarrassment they'll go through in social situations. If your shyness and anxiety becomes severe to the extent where you start panicking, then you'll find yourself struggling with social phobia.

Social phobia has been categorized in different cultures around the world as a disorder. Current estimations indicate that about 6% of the population struggle with this condition at any given time. The number of women struggling with social phobia is slightly more than men. This condition starts at a young age and develops into chronic levels later in life if left untreated.

Studies indicate that there are many people out there struggling with social phobia without knowing. Some of them seek treatment later in life after struggling with it for many years.

Anxiety is usually the predominant emotion in social phobia. This anxiety gets triggered by the fear of being humiliated and embarrassed in social situations. Getting worried that other people will evaluate you negatively makes a person become more concerned about other people's opinions about them. As a result, a person starts thinking about how to avoid the situation altogether. This, therefore, means that the main cause of nervousness before and during social situations is the fear of being evaluated negatively. We'll learn how to avoid this fear and what to do in order to replace negative thoughts with positive thoughts.

People who experience social phobia think and fear that they are being observed and watched by people who might judge them out of their actions. So they always try to stay relevant and try to impress others in order to avoid the humiliation. In most cases, they don't believe in what they are capable of. This fear makes it difficult for them to handle social situations.

It's always advisable to handle social anxiety early enough in order to stop it from developing into a life-long situation. Some people find themselves struggling with social phobia later in life because of different reasons as outlined below:

- If someone always believes that they are always anxious, they tend to develop a certain way of thinking, which makes them believe that they can't handle social situations.
- Fear and avoidance of social situations puts them in the dark, making it difficult to believe that they can become better and cope with what happens in social situations. Once a social situation is avoided for the first time, it becomes complicated and almost difficult to handle it next time.
- Belief and mentality of being terrible than other people also contribute to the fear related to social phobia. These people focus more energy

on what others think of them instead of challenging such thoughts.

- Prioritizing thoughts that will definitely lead to anxiety in social situations. For example, always believing that no matter what happens, you'll still be anxious on social occasions.

These and many other reasons contribute to development of social phobia from childhood, giving room for the condition to become a permanent problem in life. Some studies have linked social phobia to low self-esteem because individuals suffering from social anxiety always believe that they are boring, of no good when it comes to social situations. Because of continuous avoidance to tackle these beliefs, you'll find that a person struggling with social phobia always experiences anxiety during social situations.

To fight social phobia, it's always important to begin by understanding your situation and planning on what to do early enough. Almost every person struggling with this condition understands what causes their fear. To break the circle of continuous anxiety, it's important to get a clearer view of your condition so that you can embark on how to deal with it. You can make your life enjoyable again by following treatment strategies that we shall see later in this book. Understand your social phobia problem before going ahead to tackle it.

CHAPTER 2

Why do you always become anxious about social situations?

The fear of being humiliated or embarrassed is, in most cases, not recognized because patients don't usually reveal that side of their life when consulting with their doctor. Many clinicians also find it difficult to recognize this condition because, in most cases, they confuse it with normal shyness. The two are different conditions whereby one tends to be normal in life, but the other tends to become severe, denying a person the chance to enjoy life. To effectively walk out of social phobia, a patient should accept the fact that they always feel nervous when talking to people and start working on a plan that will help reduce social phobia.

Social situations that are feared by those struggling with social phobia

- Speaking in public
- Using public utilities such as toilets
- Answering questions in class

- Contributing during discussions or debates
- Drinking or eating in public
- Talking to people in authority
- Meeting new people
- Going to places that are crowded with people such as cafes or fast food joints
- Going out
- Social functions where they will be talking and meeting people

People who have social phobia will do everything possible to avoid situations listed above. In such situations, they are always concerned about being humiliated and judged wrongly. They may fear speaking in public because they believe that people will notice their shaky voice and trembling hands, which, as a result, will make them look crazy, stupid, incompetent, and unable.

This condition forces those struggling with it to avoid social situations or endure the stress that comes with this condition. When such people get exposed to the feared situations, they usually undergo anxiety response immediately, making them start developing symptoms such as blushing, nausea, stomach problems, shaky voice, trembling, and panic attacks.

This fear can develop to force a person to completely avoid certain situations and become lonely by isolating themselves.

The nature of fear and anxiety

All animals have what is known as fight or flight response, which is an automatic physiological response system. A biological explanation of this response system points out the different changes that are physiological in nature triggering the body to have extra speed and strength with a purpose of helping a person to fight a threat or escape from it by avoiding it altogether.

The changes that happen due to fight or flight response when the body detects danger or a threatening situation include:

- Becoming alert

- Increased blood pressure and heartbeat in order to increase blood supply to muscles
- When blood supply to muscles increases, it leads to sweating
- Muscles get ready for any action
- Stomach problems because digestion process slows down due to blood diversion to the heart
- Dry mouth because of a decrease in production of saliva
- Fast breathing
- Quick release of sugar from the liver for increased energy

The body normally produces adrenalin the moment it detects a threat. Once the body stops being in danger, the system cools down, and every hormone that was produced and released to the system gets metabolized, and as a result, the flight or fight response stops.

It is very common for humans to fear certain situations. When a person fears something, they normally start being anxious about it. This fear creates anxiety in mind, triggering symptoms that leave the person panicking and worried.

In people struggling with social phobia, flight or fight response helps them to escape from situations that are threatening. People who have social phobia mostly get threatened by the belief of loss of acceptance of friends or people around them. This is the main threat that makes them develop fear—but in a real sense, the disapproval may be small. This belief makes them feel that the consequences of disapproval from others will turn out being severe. This is the reason why people fearing certain social situations will do anything possible to avoid such situations days or weeks before.

Jason became anxious about making a presentation because he feared that workmates would judge him and maybe disapprove him in one way or the other. The threat that prevented Jason from making a presentation was fear of being humiliated, disapproved, or embarrassed hence he decided to avoid the presentation altogether.

You can't eliminate the response that leads to fear and anxiety. The best way to deal with this response would be to change how you interpret threatening situations. The perceived threat, in most cases, actually doesn't exist.

Panic attacks

These attacks normally start by being frightened, becoming uneasy and anxious due to a threatening situation. Panic attack symptoms can be very severe.

The following are some of the most common panic attack symptoms:

- Increased heart rate
- Blushing
- Sweating
- Shaking and trembling
- Croaking voice
- Stomach problems
- Chest pain
- Hot flushes
- Nausea
- Shortness of breath

Different people experience varying symptoms immediately after panic attacks. This, therefore, means that every individual tends to experience specific symptoms when attacked by panic. To some people, some of these symptoms may be distressing than others.

The most common symptoms people struggling with social phobia experience include sweating, shaking, and anxiety.

The feared consequences of a given situation sometimes force a person struggling with social phobia to avoid them as much as they can. If they fear that this anxiety will make others to judge or humiliate them, they will try to escape the situation. Doing this repeatedly can lead to low self-esteem, and your confidence will also be affected negatively. You'll find yourself being anxious about every social situation. Continuous avoidance of social situations can also make a person to always base their life on the need to escape these situations instead of shifting their energy toward dealing with the anxiety.

Other factors that lead to fear and anxiety

There are different factors that contribute to fear. Our lifestyles sometimes lead to fears and anxiety about social situations. If you have been drinking too much coffee or tea and smoking, this could be the reason why you are struggling with anxiety. Coffee, tea, and tobacco increase arousal and tension levels in the body because they are stimulants. These stimulants, in most cases, stimulate body responses, which, as a result, lead to anxiety and fear as we saw earlier.

The other factor that can lead to fear and anxiety of social situations is excessive consumption of alcohol. Drinking alcohol relieves a person from anxiety and fear, but this is always a false feeling, and it's never the best way to treat anxiety and fear. Relying on alcohol to relieve anxiety every time you encounter social situations can affect different organs in the body, which will result in poor health in the long run. Over-relying on alcohol to deal with your fear of social situations has no good because it only worsens your condition.

The other substance that worsens anxiety levels is smoking marijuana. Some people smoke it to help them become more relaxed, but that does not help them deal better with anxiety.

Insufficient sleep has also been found to increase anxiety and fear levels. Exhausting yourself can reduce chances of the body dealing with fear and anxiety.

If you have always struggled to be assertive over the years, then this could be one of the reasons why your fear and anxiety never stop. Studies indicate that people struggling with social phobia mostly find it difficult meeting their own needs and declining other people's demands. Being assertive can help a person to deal with their fear better than always saying yes to other people's demands.

Finally, it is important to exercise regularly to relieve your body from anxiety. Scientific findings link regular exercising to better sleep and low levels of anxiety. Exercising regularly helps improve general body health. To benefit more from exercising, you need to do it consistently.

CHAPTER 3

Social Phobia symptoms and causes

Both men and women struggle with social phobia in one way or the other. Those struggling with this condition feel shy during social situations. Some of them may have gone through anxiety at some stages in life and understand how difficult this condition can be, especially when it develops from shyness to chronic social anxiety.

Social phobia makes a person to develop a strong fear of social situations, and in most cases, this anxiety won't just go away if not dealt with appropriately and early enough. The fear also makes a person think that they will get embarrassed and humiliated.

This fear of always thinking that people will be judging you negatively prompts distressing symptoms. These symptoms make it difficult for a person to handle social situations because of fear of being embarrassed. The anxiety then makes them believe that anyone watching will definitely judge them. Here is a complete list of the most common social phobia symptoms:

- Increased heart rate/palpitations
- Blushing
- Stammering
- Shortness of breath
- Light-headedness
- Shaking
- Fear of dying
- Chills
- Hot flushes
- Unsteadiness
- Fear of going out of control
- Fear of being out of touch
- Numbness
- Sweating
- Dizziness

People struggling with social phobia without knowing sometimes find themselves drinking alcohol with an objective of reducing the symptoms. Using alcohol as an avenue of tackling social phobia can sometimes lead to excessive consumption of alcohol, which may later lead to alcoholism.

Studies indicate that social phobia can develop during adolescence in the form of being shy in simple social situations. Childhood shyness can persist and develop into social phobia through adulthood. Research indicates that about 14% of adults struggle with social phobia at some stages in life.

A high number of people struggling with social phobia become depressed at some stage in life and may also experience conditions such as panic disorder and panic attacks.

Characteristics of Social phobia

People with social phobia not only try to escape or avoid social situations. They will also try their best to avoid being criticized or noticed. They always fear answering or responding to questions during discussion or group meetings. This form of avoidance will make such people to never initiate conversations in social situations. If they get noticed during meetings, they'll almost try to be perfect or hide their fear in order not to be judged and embarrassed.

Almost everyone experiences some form of tension or anxiety in social situations. However, this fear should not get to a level where you don't enjoy life or achieve your life objectives.

Social phobia is characterized by impairment of social life, disapproval fear, fear of meeting new people and talking to them, and general avoidance of social events.

Social phobia attacks both men and women equally, despite their academic levels or experience.

How social phobia arises

So far, there is no enough evidence that can be relied upon to indicate a clear cause of social phobia. Of course there are different speculations by different schools of thought linking this condition to the brain and physiological body responses.

Find below a list of suggestions by different studies trying to explain causes of social phobia:

- **Imitations**: It is believed that people can develop social phobia through imitation. For instance, children can develop social phobia if their parents show symptoms. Some students can also develop social phobia if their teacher avoids social situations such as meeting parents.

- **Upbringing:** Children who fail to learn certain social skills at a tender age may end up developing shyness and social phobia in life. These children then grow without being taught how to handle social situations, making them develop anxiety whenever asked to do a small talk or respond to questions.

- **Physiological factors:** Continuous anxiety triggered by response factors can also lead to social phobia. Threatening situations may sometimes trigger flight or fight response which leads to fear and anxiety.

Social phobia is a mental condition. Like many mental conditions linked to the brain, social phobia results from different environmental and genetic interactions. If you suspect that you could be having this condition, the best thing to do is to talk to a doctor. This way, you'll be able to know your condition better.

Social phobia affects people in different ways. The symptoms vary from one person to the next. Despite the difficult situations a person experiences, the good thing is that it can be treated. This can only be achieved by sticking to working strategies, as we shall see later in this book.

CHAPTER 4

Feeling anxious in public

The key part of social phobia is the fear of being embarrassed and evaluated negatively by people around you. The person who has social phobia worries that they may end up doing something that will make them embarrassed. This fear may come as a result of a specific situation or, in most cases, in social situations.

This fear may be so intense that people who have social phobia may end up missing going to work, school, or social places. These people often start fearing about social situations days before. This makes them to devise strategies that can help them escape the fear. This fear sometimes pushes them toward depression and, in some cases, low self-esteem.

People struggling with social phobia may sometimes have twisted thoughts—negative thoughts and false belief—about how other people will see them. This is why they often fear certain social situations before they happen. This then leads to a vicious cycle of anxiety affecting daily performance and ability to hit daily targets.

Social phobia in public can sometimes lead to performance anxiety whereby a person does not feel anxious in social situations but fears performing, giving a speech, dancing or singing in public, playing a game.

This fear normally starts in childhood all the way through adulthood. Without early treatment, this condition can last for years and always affect a person's life negatively on a daily basis. People who have social phobia develop fear, which makes it difficult for them to be around people, and always develop anxiety every time they meet people.

If you are struggling with social phobia, you'll find yourself going through a lot of stress due to the fear of appearing in public, and in some cases, this anxiety maybe too much for a person to handle. The things that people consider normal will not look normal to you. Things like eye contact and conversations will always make you feel uncomfortable if you have social phobia. This phobia can lead to the social side of your life falling apart because you can't just see things from the same side like others.

One of the most common mental conditions is social phobia. Not so many people find it easy asking for help the moment they realize that they are struggling with the condition. However, you should not give up if you are struggling with social phobia. You can be treated and become the person you've always wanted to be. If you feel that your shyness has escalated to a point where you always try to avoid social situations, it is advisable to find help in different treatment options available.

People experience social phobia in different ways. The most troubling situations include: attending parties, starting conversations, talking and meeting strangers, dating, maintaining eye contact, using public toilets, public speaking, eating and drinking in front of people.

As we saw earlier, some of these situations cannot pose a threat to you. For instance, some people will find it easy going to a social situation but difficult to give a speech. Every person struggling with social phobia has different reasons for fearing certain social situations. However, all social-phobic people fear embarrassment and humiliation, offending people, being watched doing something, and being judged.

What does it feel like experiencing social phobia?

Every person struggling with social phobia goes through a different experience in social situations. Most of them experience stomach problems, sweating, blushing, increased heart rate, and tension.

The symptoms that these people feel may start days before an event or moments to a social situation. After the event, a person may spend time wondering how they acted or performed during an event.

People who always fear social events, in most cases, dwell upon the possibility of some form of danger.

This form of worry creates a vicious cycle and a tendency of basing their thoughts on negative events, leading to symptoms such as increased heart rate and sweating.

Obviously, when anxiety and tension is too high, our performance tends to never remain the same. Anxiety always has a negative impact on performance. However, according to scientific findings, moderate fear and anxiety can be helpful because anxiety sometimes helps human beings to prepare how to deal with danger. Moderate anxiety can motivate you to defend yourself against threats, put more effort, and prepare for challenges early.

Fear affects people struggling with social phobia in the form of emotions when they start imagining some form of danger or when they are confronted with threats. This anxiety or fear leads to a psychological reaction that happens almost immediately with one intention—to have the person avoid or escape the threat as fast as possible. This fear leads the body to an immediate overdrive to ensure that it avoids the threat. Blood supply to muscles increases when physiological changes occur in the body. Breathing rate also increases to supply more oxygen to different parts of the body.

All the physiological responses that occur in the body when it detects danger or a threat are all meant to help it escape it. If this happens to people who do not understand how to manage this fear, they end up avoiding situations that are threatening.

The clinical term of becoming anxious and fearful about social situations is known as panic attack. This fear takes over a person even when the perceived social situation presents no danger.

Social phobia intensity varies from one person to the next. Some people experience manageable fear while others experience intense fear, which ends up overwhelming them, leading to symptoms of anxiety and fear that we have already covered in preceding chapters of this book.

Psychological fear and anxiety can make you feel out of touch with yourself and lead to severe symptoms like becoming crazy or developing a fear of dying.

No matter how you experience fear or anxiety, the good news is that it can be treated, and the most important thing to do is to have hope during the whole process.

CHAPTER 5

Nature of Social phobia

Social phobia attacks people in different ways. It can be in the form of fear of a certain social situation or an event perceived to be a threat. A person may fear not hitting a target or have a fear of being unable to meet goals or fear of being judged.

Anxiety is usually associated with physiological changes in the body such as flight or fight response when a person suddenly thinks of a threatening situation or something perceived to be dangerous.

Social anxiety or social phobia is triggered by unrecognized threats or guesses that make a person feel that they'll embarrass themselves by doing things in public. For instance, a person may be anxious about being judged by others or humiliated by performing or talking to an audience. Anxiety is usually linked with vague feelings of something dangerous happening.

Anxiety can have a physiological impact on the body in the form of increased heart rate, tension, sweating, increased breathing rate, and dry mouth. Anxiety can as well interfere with our ability to express our feelings, including the way we act and deal with some simple situations in life. Anxiety can be severe to an extent where it can make a person come up with a strategy that can help them avoid appearing in public, pushing them into isolation.

For a person to recover fully from social phobia, the treatment program must be able to deal with the condition on three different levels:

1. Physiological level
2. Avoidance of social situations
3. Change of perceptions about certain social situations

Later in this book, we shall look at various social phobia treatment options that have been found to be effective.

Becoming anxious can be triggered by thinking of a particularly threatening situation crossing your mind.

When you begin fearing and getting stressed about what that particular threatening situation holds, you start experiencing symptoms.

Life is full of challenges on a daily basis, and evading anxiety is sometimes impossible. It's normal to become anxious about certain situations in life because that's how our bodies are designed. However, this anxiety shouldn't prevent a person from doing certain things in life.

The purpose of this book is to help anyone struggling with anxiety in life. Anxiety can be controlled by following treatment options which we shall look at later in this book. If you are one the 7% of the population that is struggling with social phobia, all you have to do to get back your social life is to do exactly what this book suggests and consult a mental health specialist to give you further instructions.

CHAPTER 6

Types of social phobia

Social phobia is a common condition which currently affects over 15 million people in the US. Most of them developed this condition at an early age. People struggling with social phobia disorder always experience anxiety and worry about appearing in social situations. They always fear being judged and embarrassed in public. The fear attacks them in different ways with different symptoms, but the most common ones are sweating, trembling, increase in heart rate, among others.

These people are always self-conscious and fear being humiliated in public. People struggling with this condition always ignore talking about it. That's probably the reason why many social phobia patients rarely talk about their situation, making it hard for doctors to identify the problem and diagnose it.

The truth about social phobia is that it is important to seek help from your doctor. This book takes you through different topics about social phobia and the strategies that can be used to overcome the persistent, overwhelming and unreasonable anxiety caused by this condition.

The moment you realize that you've started developing social phobia, it is important to treat it early enough. The more you ignore treating it, the more it becomes difficult to deal with. Some people become anxious and shy in social situations while young, but the condition improves as a person grows older. For some few individuals, social phobia can become part of life if not treated early enough.

Studies show that different factors in life can lead to social phobia becoming a life-long issue in some people. If someone finds it easy avoiding social situations, this affects the person in such a way that they won't even try to cope and find out whether they can comfortably handle social situations. This avoidance sticks on their mind, and next time there is a social situation, the first thing they will do is to avoid it all together.

People who always listen to their fears, in most cases, develop this kind of personality which won't just allow them to even try and overcome the anxiety. This then becomes a vicious cycle, and the mind makes them believe that they are no good when meeting people or talking to them.

Tackling social phobia takes a lot, and if social phobia treatment strategies are followed, patients can actually benefit a lot. The mind is a very important social phobia treatment tool that patients should learn how to work with in order to stop social phobia from denying them a quality life.

That being said, let's now look at the different types of social phobia.

Types of social phobia

There are normally two types of social phobia, namely, general social phobia and specific general phobia.

General social phobia

General social phobia won't just let you attend social events or go to places that are crowded—like eating places or halls. To be specific enough, it can be particularly difficult for someone struggling with general social phobia to attend parties. It makes you think whether or not to go to a party. If you finally attend the party, you'll still feel uncomfortable being around people, and the anxiety will give you a false impression that everyone is looking at what you do. People with general social phobia, in some cases, may have to drink alcohol before going to a party in order to relax and make them feel better.

If you have general social phobia, you:

- Find it hard to go to restaurants and shops
- Fear that everyone is looking at what you do
- Hate meeting people
- Fear drinking and eating where people are
- Can't let people down or disappoint them

If you feel any of the above symptoms, then chances are high that you have general social phobia. Just like any other type of social anxiety, general social phobia affects people negatively and prevents them from reaching full potential.

Specific social phobia

Specific social phobia mostly affects people who are always the center of attention such as speakers, actors, teachers, salespeople, and many more. This type of social phobia allows an individual to mingle and socialize with people freely without any fear.

So where exactly does specific social phobia come in?

Since socializing is never a problem for a person struggling with specific social phobia, the problem comes in when they have to talk in front of others. A person struggling with this type of social phobia will start trembling, sweating, and will experience increased heart rate and breathing when asked to perform or talk.

Specific social phobia knows no one. It will attack even the most respected and experienced people when asked to speak to others. This type of phobia will also make it difficult to ask a question in public even for the most experienced speakers.

Specific social phobia creates anxiety and fear which can't allow a person to make a speech, to talk, to dance or perform in front of people. This happens because they fear and don't believe in what they can do. Such people fear being seen incompetent.

Symptoms of both types of social phobia discussed above are somehow similar because, in both types of social phobia, a person may experience sweating, increased heart rate, dry mouth, stomach problems, numbness, and increased breathing. In some cases, the symptoms can worsen the anxiety and fear experienced in social situations.

These types of social phobia affect both men and women. Studies show that more women than men struggle with social phobia. However, more men than women seek treatment for social phobia according to current standing figures. The reason behind this is not yet known.

CHAPTER 7

Effects of social phobia

Social anxiety definitely has a negative impact on quality of life. For a person struggling with social anxiety, regular social situations trigger anxiety and self-consciousness, which pushes them into isolation. They will always come up with excuses in order to avoid social situations. They may not even be able to eat or drink in public, let alone attending a party.

Social phobia can sometimes lead to disconnectedness and loneliness for people who prefer isolating themselves and avoiding social events. The fear and anxiety commonly felt by individuals who have social phobia is always intense than normal nervousness or fear of certain situations.

If a person who has social phobia continuously isolates themselves from social events, every aspect of their relationships at home, school, or work gets affected negatively. This is why it's always advisable to find help early enough before it becomes chronic.

This condition also makes people experience subjective suffering if left without treatment. A prolonged struggle with this condition can, therefore, impact negatively on a person's social life and general performance.

Some social anxiety sufferers who can't handle the fear of appearing in social events sometimes drink in order to feel comfortable and relaxed when going to social situations. As a result, this may lead to alcoholism, and those who depend on drugs may find themselves getting addicted.

Once social phobia conquers every aspect of a person's life, it becomes difficult for that person to enjoy life with friends, schoolmates, relatives, and family members.

Struggling with social anxiety can severely limit your ability to enjoy daily life. This condition will not only interfere with your social life alone but also affect you psychologically. The secret is to always look for the right treatment before the situation worsens.

You may not fully understand how this condition affects your loved one, but it is always good to help them in any way possible so that they can conquer it and get back their life.

Psychological impacts

This condition mostly involves fear of social situations. If you are struggling with it, it is important to know how you are supposed to confront it. It can lead to psychological torture if it becomes part of life and left untreated. Some of the psychological effects a person struggling with social phobia is likely to experience include depression, self-consciousness, low self-esteem, intense fear, panic attacks, negative thoughts, and feelings of inferiority.

Social phobia can also have some devastating impacts on a person's relationship and social life. For instance, it can lead to difficulty maintaining relationships, going to social events such as parties or functions, low self-esteem which will cause family and marital feuds, low performance, and loneliness caused by anxiety and shyness.

Economic effects

Many countries took a long time to recognize social phobia as a health condition that affected a large number of their population. These countries initially under-treated this condition before they came to realize that it actually had an adverse impact on their economy.

Studies indicate that socio-phobic individuals have a lower household income and are less likely to be found in high socioeconomic categories. These people also experience lower employment rate compared to those who do not struggle with the condition. This, as a result, leads to indirect or direct negative impacts on the general economy.

CHAPTER 8

Strategies for self-help

It takes a lot for one to conquer social phobia. This book has outlined key strategies to help anyone struggling with social phobia.

Step 1: Understanding social phobia

Understanding social phobia is a crucial step because you'll be able to learn the reason behind the fear and anxiety felt in social situations. Understand the anxiety and learn to look at it from a different perspective.

As we saw earlier, anxiety is a normal thing that helps the body in a variety of ways like preparing for danger or a threatening situation. The objective here would then be to learn how to manage it and not avoid it. When the body senses danger, a physiological process is triggered immediately to help the body prepare well. For example, the heart will pump blood very fast to energize muscles when there is a threat.

It's also important to learn and understand that sometimes anxiety and fear can be problematic when your body tells you that there is a threat when there is actually no threat.

Feeling anxious in front of people is a regular thing in human beings. However, it becomes a problem when the fear and anxiety grows to prevent you from reaching full potential. The strategies outlined in this book will help you manage your fear well and prevent anxiety from becoming a problem in life.

Step 2: Strategies

To help you get rid of social phobia and fear of social situations, there are strategies that have been found to work.

Strategy 1: Observe your fears and anxiety

All social phobia books recommend this as the first step toward controlling your fear of social situations. Social phobia makes a person to develop a fear of social situations like talking in class, verbal contribution during a discussion, attending parties, and many other social events. These situations will lead to a person experiencing symptoms such as sweating, stomach problems, blushing, shaky voice, and high heart rate.

TIP: If you feel these symptoms in social situations, it is important to take time and relax so that you can find out and list all the situations that make you develop the symptoms listed above. Understand what causes your social phobia. List all the symptoms that you go through in different social situations. Understanding your fears is the best way to help you manage it well.

You can as well use a simple strategy such as listing your anxiety and symptoms on a table against the dates you experienced fear. Look at the following example:

Date	Event	Symptom
8/8/17	Meeting my wife's parents	Sweating, stomach problems,

| 12/12/17 | Attending a party | Blushing, high heart rate |

The essence of this kind of a table is to help you monitor social situations that make you experience different social phobia symptoms.

Strategy 2: Relax

Relaxing is an essential anxiety management tool. Try to relax when feeling anxious. This helps a lot in containing the fear. By relaxing, you allow your body to contain the symptoms and reduce the effects of these symptoms when facing social situations.

Breathe slowly

Try to be calm and reduce your breathing rate. When confronted with threatening situations, we usually experience fast breathing rate, making it difficult to even think, let alone facing social situations. Breathe slowly in order to reduce the impacts of your fear of social situations.

This strategy, in most cases, acts as a foundation for anxiety management. It's a tool to help in thinking straight and calming your fear. Breathing slowly is a technique which has been found to be helpful in managing anxiety over the years. Avoid over-breathing as much as you can and try smooth and light breaths through your nose. You should not be worried about someone noticing your breathing because, in most cases, breathing through the nose is unnoticeable.

Maintain this breathing strategy everytime you feel anxious until you feel better and relaxed. In some cases, you may still feel social phobia symptoms even after breathing and calming. If you experience this, just maintain breathing slowly until you feel better.

If, for the first time, this breathing strategy doesn't give you a calming effect in managing anxiety, you can try to avoid getting focused on it and try to do it regularly. Do not always think about it being the main anxiety management tool. Allow it to come naturally and relax.

Relaxing

Another important strategy that allows the body to relax when faced with anxiety and fear. Relaxing your muscles will help reduce tension related to fear and anxiety.

The tension a person experiences can be psychological or physical. When you allow your body to relax, the nerves also cease, sending certain signals to the brain, which, as a result, calms the body naturally.

Biologically, our muscles are meant to relax if they are not required to help different body parts to perform. Prolonged exposure to stressing situations may sometimes make muscles to maintain high tension and lead to fatigue, pains in the muscles, and sometimes headaches. If muscles get exposed to high tension, this condition may result in some forms of irritability and unease, making the body prone to anxiety attacks. This gets worse when a person starts thinking about a threatening situation like speaking at a social function or meeting people.

This process, as a result, leads to panic attacks, making it hard to encounter social situations. To manage your anxiety after a panic attack, it is important to allow your muscles to relax. By relaxing, you allow the body to reduce production of hormones that increase physiological response triggered by a threatening situation.

By allowing your muscles to relax, you reduce chances of experiencing excess arousal. You also manage to cope well when faced with a challenging situation.

TIP: Learn to allow your muscles to relax when faced with a challenging situation for you to manage it well

Muscle relaxation and breathing techniques are strategies that have been found to work in dealing with social phobia symptoms. You can use other strategies like exercising, getting enough sleep, and minimizing environmental factors that trigger anxiety.

Strategy 3: Positive thinking

In most cases, people struggling with social phobia experience negative thinking like fear or being judged and humiliated by others. They tend to believe that something negative will happen to them or they might end up embarrassing themselves in social situations.

Such thoughts always leave them thinking that:

- They will end up saying something stupid

- People will laugh at them
- People will notice their fear
- They will be boring or miss something to say
- Nobody will talk to them or like what they say

If your mind always thinks that social situations are dangerous, then chances are that you will fear and become anxious. The mind could be lying to you that these situations are dangerous. Do not allow what your mind believes about social situations to prevent you from enjoying life. Try to learn how to think positively about social situations in order to manage your anxiety well.

To assess thoughts that cross your mind about social situations, you can list them and find how you can substitute them with positive thoughts.

How to substitute negative mentality with positive mentality:

Start by answering the following question: What do you think or fear might happen to you in social events or situations? The answer to this can either be

"Saying something that might embarrass me" or "Being boring." List everything you are afraid of so as to understand all your fears. Understand your fears and try to go through the list regularly to better understand your situation well.

Regular evaluation of your thoughts should be the next step after understanding your fears. You should also know that whatever your mind thinks about social situations are just guesses and not facts. Let your mind come up with facts and not guesses.

Your personal assessment questions

1. How sure am I that this will happen?
2. Is this the first time this will happen?
3. Is my thought right about it?
4. Do I have to find it difficult being assertive?
5. What might happen after this?

Whatever your mind tells you about social situations are just guesses.

Remember, you are not the first or last person to make a mistake, and you don't have to please everyone or strive to be perfect.

This assessment will open your mind and see things from the actual side of life. You'll also realize that the things that your mind makes you afraid of are just guesses or exaggerations.

Strategy 4: Facing anxiety

Don't rely on a short-term strategy of avoiding social situations. This doesn't help at all. Look for a long-term strategy that will help you conquer anxiety. Avoiding situations will prevent you from seeing facts about what makes you anxious. Postponing a problem doesn't solve it at all.

Use strategies 1, 2, and 3 discussed above to face your fears and manage anxiety. Managing your anxiety and facing your fears head-on helps you long-term.

Just as we saw earlier in this chapter, you can manage your fears by listing what worries you most about social events. To face your anxiety, it is recommended that you list all the things that you are worried about. Maybe it could be talking to leaders or greeting a workmate. After listing your fears, start practicing and taking them head-on everyday. For example, you can start with greeting your workmates daily, and you'll find your fear reducing with time.

Repeat the same process with everything that makes you afraid, and you'll find yourself free from anxiety before you know it.

After taking care of things that make you feel anxious, it may be good to start making new friends and improving your social relationships.

Go to social places and expand your network by making new friends. Develop new social skills that can boost your confidence in making friends. You can socialize with people in different places like organizations and clubs, at work, school, and sports arena. You can also register at local volunteer institutions to help you meet people in places such as hospitals and community centers.

After following these self-assessment strategies in countering your fears, you'll definitely start seeing some improvement. Encourage yourself, even if it means going through stressing situations on the journey of conquering social phobia.

Remain focused and be consistent in what this book suggests in order to start enjoying life. Do not forget that you can only achieve your goal through hard work and consistency. Whatever you do, just make sure that the strategies you use can help you manage your anxiety and fear of social situations. To help yourself better, it would be right doing what this book suggests and seeing a therapist to guide you further on how to overcome social phobia. Avoiding social situations altogether does not help you at all. In fact, it worsens your fear of social situations and prolongs the problem.

CHAPTER 9

Frequency of Social Phobia

Approximately 9% of youths and 14% of adults in the US struggle with social anxiety at some point in life. According to a study by National Comorbidity Survey, adolescents in the age bracket of 13 to 18 struggling with social phobia experience the following fears in social situations:

- Making new friends in the same age bracket
- Dating
- Talking to leaders or those in authority
- Going to a party with people in the same age bracket
- Going into crowded places
- Places where people will see them do something
- Talking to strangers.

Internationally, social phobia prevalence stands between 7% and 12%. In many countries, doctors find it difficult diagnosing social phobia in patients who fail to talk about their anxiety. This mostly happens in patients struggling with conditions such as depression.

Patients diagnosed with social phobia may sometimes be diagnosed with a different anxiety disorder due to its comorbid nature. One study revealed that about 10% of people struggling with social phobia had a different anxiety disorder like specific or generalized social phobia disorder. Social phobia can also affect occupational and educational functioning in adults. Adults struggling with this condition, in most cases, find it difficult making new friends or maintaining relationships.

This condition affects both men and women, but it's more frequent in women than men. Despite the high number of women struggling with social phobia than men, more men than women seek treatment.

According to different scientific studies about anxiety, social phobia is one of the most persistent conditions linked to anxiety. Despite the high number of those struggling with this condition in the community, only half of them seek medical help. They go for treatment after struggling with the condition for many years. The chances of successfully treating social phobia at an early age are high compared to dealing with it after becoming chronic.

This condition can be treated effectively, but the lack of information and awareness among the population has made it difficult for recognition of this condition. It's a condition which has received under-recognition in many countries despite a huge number of people struggling with it.

Different studies connect this condition to low-self-esteem. Those struggling with the condition find it difficult starting conversations or contributing during discussions at school, places of work or social situations. The continuous vicious cycle of avoiding social situations makes it become a long-term problem in a person's life, preventing them from enjoying life.

A number of strategies, as discussed in this book, can be used in overcoming and preventing social phobia. Dealing with this condition requires a person to avoid being too focused on personal life, avoiding negative thinking, dealing with avoidance of social situations, understanding your condition, and dealing with symptoms related to social phobia.

Use the strategies recommended in the previous chapter to help you manage anxiety and understand your fears well. Even if you find yourself struggling with social phobia, you should not give up. Find the right strategy capable of giving you results as discussed in this book. The earlier you deal with social phobia, the better. The other important thing to note is that there's no need to avoid situations that your mind guesses to be threatening. Confronting what your mind believes to be dangerous is the right way to cope with situations that make you feel anxious.

CHAPTER 10

Treatment options

Just like any other health condition, the first step toward treatment of social phobia is to see a doctor to help in diagnosing it. After seeing a doctor or a specialist in mental health, you'll be able to know the level of your condition and the necessary steps needed in treatment. There are normally two main psychotherapy treatment options for social phobia. These are cognitive behavioral therapy and medication. Let's start by understanding cognitive behavioral therapy.

Cognitive-behavioral therapy (CBT)

The aim of this form of therapy is to help a patient struggling with social phobia to replace thoughts that make them fear social situations with constructive and helpful thoughts. This can be achieved through a mental support program.

Through cognitive behavior therapy, a patient learns positive ways of thinking, reacting to social situations, and behaving in a way that can make them feel better and less fearful.

Through cognitive-behavioral therapy, a patient learns how to deal with negative thoughts, how to identify negative thoughts, and how to replace these thoughts with constructive thoughts for long-term benefits in addressing social phobia.

A person struggling with social phobia sometimes experiences fear in the presence of others. This fear varies from one person to the next in terms of intensity of the anxiety felt. The intensity of the fear also depends on a situation provoking it. Overcoming social phobia requires an in-depth understanding of thoughts and fear that triggers symptoms discussed earlier in this book. After understanding your thoughts, you'll be able to see your anxiety from a clearer angle and plan how to manage it.

Many social phobia books refer to these thoughts as cognitions which should be dealt with constructively in order to avoid social phobia and its impacts on life.

Whatever happens during social situation does not create the anxiety that people struggling with social phobia generally feel. What actually leads to fear are the thoughts that are at the back of our mind in the form of guesses. You'll definitely feel anxious if you always think that people will judge you or you may embarrass yourself.

The problem here is the way we look at things and not the situation itself. The secret to successful cognitive therapy lies in the way we interpret situations. The interpretations are, in most cases, influenced by the way we dealt with previous similar situations. For example, if you always avoid and escape social situations every time because of fear of being humiliated, there is no possibility that your thoughts about social situations will change next time you encounter a similar situation. If you always set your mind in such a way that it gets used to avoiding social situations because you fear embarrassing yourself, there is no way it will cease looking at social situations as a threat if you don't change the way you look at things. If you've always looked at social situations from a negative point of view, you must change your thoughts in order to benefit from cognitive therapy, despite its effectiveness in the treatment of social phobia.

If you always find yourself extremely anxious and fearful, there is a possibility you are negatively interpreting social events. If you always consider yourself boring and of no good when it comes to social situations, you need to stop that mentality and start looking at yourself as capable of handling social situations, no matter what. Your thoughts about social situations could just be guesses and not facts. So don't believe in them.

Cognitive therapy is meant to help us examine thoughts about certain situations. After identifying and examining our thoughts about these situations, we should substitute them with constructive and positive thinking.

It takes some practice changing the way you view things. The best way to approach this would be through phases such as:

- Understanding your thoughts about certain situations
- Deciding whether you need to continue thinking the same
- Looking at the thoughts differently and restructuring them to be helpful to your situation
- Practicing helpful thoughts

What are your thoughts?

Tracking down thoughts that cross our minds about certain situations can be difficult because this normally happens automatically. The different categories of these thoughts are:

Automatic: These thoughts just cross our minds without knowing it.

Involuntary: These thoughts just come into our minds, and ignoring can be difficult at times.

Unhelpful: These thoughts make you fear a situation more and always prevent a person from reaching their full potential.

By practicing in phases and identifying these thoughts, one can benefit a lot in fighting social phobia. You can start identifying these thoughts by using what you normally feel when anxious or worried. For instance, you can assess thoughts that constantly make you feel uneasy.

You may as well relax and ask yourself the things that are making you anxious or the feelings that are making you uncomfortable. Doing this regularly will definitely help you at the end of the process of dealing with social phobia. You'll find yourself with a list of thoughts that make you feel anxious and worried. Once you manage to identify them, you'll now start dealing with them one after the other by replacing negatives with positives.

What next after identifying thoughts?

Once you identify the thoughts, the next step should be transforming them into constructive and realistic thinking. Examine the thoughts deeply and in a logical way. This process involves challenging the thoughts one after the other to find out if they are actual representations of a social situation.

Examples of questions to use in challenging these thoughts

1. Will it actually happen the way I think?
2. What other option exists?
3. How serious are the impacts?
4. What made me think this way?

Answer these questions well and repeat the same process every time you become anxious about certain situations in life.

After challenging and analyzing your way of thinking, you'll come to realize that some of the thoughts that lead to anxiety do not actually reflect what will happen.

Always remember that thoughts that make you fear social situations do not exactly mean that you'll be judged or humiliated. People will be more interested in other positive things and not judging or humiliating you.

Exposure

To overcome social phobia, it is important to try and face the situations that make you feel anxious. You can start by imagining that you've already faced the situations before going ahead to actually face it. For instance, if speaking in front of a large group of people makes you feel anxious, you can start by having a small talk with a friend and gradually increase the number of people you talk to.

By doing this, you'll get exposed to almost a similar situation to what makes you anxious. From there, you can identify your thoughts and challenge them one after the other, replacing them with realistic thoughts.

For exposure method to work in the treatment of social phobia, it is important to start with the least fear-provoking thoughts or situations before tackling difficult and complex situations. Many social phobia books and studies indicate that exposure is a potent tool in the treatment of social phobia.

Importance of exposure

As we saw earlier, there are different types of social phobia, namely, generalized social phobia and specific social phobia. People struggling with social phobia normally develop a fear of certain social situations either by thinking about those situations or by being in them. Something as small as thinking about social situations that make them anxious is enough to trigger flight or fight response, which, as a result, leads to symptoms of social phobia. This response makes the body to naturally try and avoid such situations all together hence reducing the fear and anxiety.

It's so unfortunate that this vicious cycle of avoiding certain situations causing anxiety and fear leads to social phobia. Continuously avoiding social situations because of fear of being judged by others makes a person miss a chance to disapprove the negative thoughts lying at the back of their mind.

By avoiding social situations, your negative thoughts get strengthened daily, making it difficult to confront these situations.

Medication

Medication is another social phobia treatment option that has been found to work well. The most common medications used in the treatment of social phobia are antidepressants and anti-anxiety drugs. There are different types of anti-anxiety drugs that are normally used in the treatment of social phobia. These medications are usually potent and effective in dealing with anxiety. Some of these medications will start working immediately and should not be used for long in most cases.

Antidepressant drugs are mostly used in the treatment of depression but can as well be used in the treatment of social phobia. For a person struggling with social phobia, they may have to take antidepressants for weeks before seeing results. Some antidepressant drugs have side effects such as insomnia, nausea, headache, and unease. However, these side effects can be contained and minimized by starting with low doses, as you increase with time. In case of any side effects, the best thing to do would be to talk to your mental health specialist.

It is important to note that antidepressants can sometimes be risky for some people, and that is why you should consult your doctor before going ahead to use them. These drugs can be risky for young adults and children.

Studies indicate that the use of antidepressants or anti-anxiety treatment alongside psychotherapy treatment such as cognitive behavior therapy can help reduce symptoms related to social phobia.

Different studies indicate that the most effective social phobia treatment option is cognitive behavior therapy (CBT). If your treatment option doesn't work as fast as you thought, don't just give up. Continue following different psychotherapy strategies outlined in this book, and you'll find yourself free from social phobia before you know it. Social phobia treatment is generalized and not specific. Every patient experiences different social phobia symptoms. Expect to go through some trial and error in your social phobia treatment journey. If a certain treatment option worked for somebody, it does not mean that it will also work for you.

Beta blockers are also another social phobia treatment option. Beta blockers as a form of social phobia treatment reduce the impacts of adrenaline. They are very effective in reduction of heart rate, blood pressure, and breathing rate. It is advisable to take these drugs early enough to find out whether or not you can benefit from them.

This form of medication helps in reducing the impacts of social phobia symptoms such as sweating, increased heart rate, and shaking. This medication is ideal for individuals struggling with social phobia, especially when it comes to social situations that require them to perform, talk, or give a speech.

Some patients discontinue medication after symptoms reduce within a short time of treatment. However, some patients may have to continue using medication for years to achieve full treatment and avoid relapse. Some people get help through medication while others get it through CBT. In some cases, a combination of different treatment options also works well in the treatment of social phobia and reduction of its symptoms.

To benefit from different social phobia treatment options, it is advisable to stick to the right medication and follow the instructions and guidelines by your mental health specialist.

When it comes to treatment of social phobia using medications, it is very important to consult with your mental health specialist. This is very important because your mental health specialist will be able to recommend the best treatment combination and give you further advice. Your mental health specialist is the right person to help you understand the right treatment option.

Social phobia affects people in different ways in terms of the symptoms felt. The treatment options discussed in this chapter have been found to be very effective in dealing with social phobia, but as a person struggling with the condition, it is important to seek medical help early enough to be able to contain it.

CHAPTER 11

Dealing with relapse

The term relapse describes the experience a person goes through after achieving improved ways of thinking or conquering social phobia after treatment. It may lead to difficulties coping with events that happen in daily life. It is important to understand what may happen after a period of improved thinking and after following social phobia treatment.

Setbacks are very common, and this can happen to any person trying to recover from social phobia. While some people understand how to deal with relapse, others may find it difficult going through it. It's discouraging and devastating at the same time when you have to go back to a frustrating situation after putting effort and using relevant resources to recover.

In this chapter, we shall look at how to deal with relapse and help you develop a strategy to prevent it. After taking your time to treat social phobia and getting rid of destructive or negative thoughts, you'll start feeling better with improved thinking and in a better position to deal with anxiety. In this chapter, you'll be able to learn how to maintain this improvement and become stronger in terms of the way you deal with fear or anxiety.

By comprehending thoughts that trigger your anxiety, having a solid plan, and making good use of social phobia treatment strategies, a person can reduce the chances of a relapse.

Causes of relapse

There are many factors that have been found to lead to relapses. Some of them include negative thoughts, events, and objects. These triggers can sometimes make a person to experience social phobia symptoms. Some of these triggers happen in a quick manner before knowing that they are actually happening. Identifying the triggers that lead to symptoms after recovery from social phobia can sometimes be difficult for some people.

The following have been found to be the main relapse triggers among those recovering from social phobia and other conditions related to anxiety:

- Events in life (such as divorce)
- Stopping medication
- Becoming ill
- Falling sick
- Stress
- Arguments

It is important to identify your triggers in order to be in a better position to deal with them once you experience them next time. Try to figure out what your triggers could be and make a list.

Identifying changes

Sometimes changes happen without realizing, and this is why some people find it difficult listing changes that have happened in social phobia treatment. The easiest way of finding changes that have happened is by comparing the past with the present. Compare the way you feel now and how you felt in the past. By doing this, you will be able to notice improvements.

Use the following examples to help you find out changes:

- How have my thoughts changed?
- What different feelings do I have?
- Am I acting differently?
- Is there a difference in the way I handle friends?

These questions will help you identify different changes in order to be able to keep or drop some of them:

- What led to changes in my thoughts?
- What led to changes in the way I act?
- What should I do to apply the changes that have occurred?
- Have I gained positive skills to help me?
- How do I apply the changes in my life?

After finding the changes that have happened in your life, the next thing to do would be to look at them from a different view to help you confront what you need to drop or maintain.

Identifying relapse signs

Some people experience relapse despite identifying different factors that trigger it. After learning how to identify changes, the next thing is to find out signs that a relapse has occurred. So, what are the signs?

Changes in sleeping cycle

If you find it difficult to wake up early in the morning or if you have not been getting enough sleep at night, chances are that you are relapsing. The other sign of relapse could also be if you have been worrying about your sleep. Usually, when a person starts being anxious, they will start worrying about sleep quality.

Changes in your feelings

Some of the common signs of a relapse include sudden changes in mood, experiencing panic attacks and changes in feelings. Experiencing negative thoughts could be an indication that your mood has changed hence signaling a possibility of a relapse.

Behavioral change

Changes in behavior that indicate the possibility of a relapse can sometimes be in the form of things associated with anxiety. This can include withdrawal from social situations or avoiding social contact with some people.

Changes in our thoughts

If you start thinking negatively and fearing certain situations because your mind tells you that people might judge your actions, then this could be a sign of a relapse.

Other signs of a relapse include sudden changes in irritability, symptoms, and poor concentration. When a relapse occurs, some people find it difficult to concentrate even on simple assignments. This lack of concentration could be as a result of distractions or unsettled mind. When the mind races, leading to poor concentrations, a person may become anxious about a social situation they consider to be a threat.

Key factors in prevention of a relapse

Anxiety can be managed and controlled in many effective ways. Important factors in the prevention of a relapse include good health, positive thinking, exercising on a regular basis, eating a balanced diet, getting sound and enough sleep, and many more.

Maintaining good mental and body health is very important in managing the anxiety we sometimes face in life.

How to deal with a relapse

It can be a bit scary and disappointing to experience a relapse. Managing a relapse starts with noticing the signs and coming up with a strategy to prevent going back.

By identifying the signs of a relapse, you'll be able to come up with a strategy to help you control the situation and prevent the signs of experiencing symptoms.

To prevent a relapse from happening, you need to control your anxiety first and be positive about your prevention plan.

First, you need to believe in your relapse prevention strategy. Secondly, split the plan into steps that will help control your panic or fear.

You can start by assessing your thoughts to find out what improves your feeling or mood. Identify positive thoughts that can help you feel better and manage anxiety. Anytime negative thoughts cross your mind, you can replace them with constructive thoughts to help control your anxiety better.

Another strategy would be to control yourself every time you realize that you've begun avoiding social situations or withdrawing from relationships. Try as much as possible to continue being positive and always maintain your social relationships every time you get tempted to avoid social situations.

Recommendations

All social phobia treatment strategies explained in this book should be practiced—even after noticing improvement—in order to help minimize chances of a relapse. A person may also have to avoid some things in life in order to recover fully and avoid a relapse. For instance, it's advisable to avoid smoking, drinking alcohol, and using substances that contain stimulants.

Maintain a balanced diet to continue being healthy and for the brain to get sufficient energy for better and improved thinking. When the body is healthy, it manages anxiety well and prepares well in case of anxiety.

Don't forget exercising regularly for your mental health. You can always exercise in the gym or by taking a walk. Sleep is also a crucial factor in dealing with social phobia and preventing a relapse. It is advisable to get enough sleep, which, as a result, will help our thoughts in different positive ways.

Sometimes it is important to look for strategies that can help us manage social anxiety better. For example, if you find it difficult managing anxiety after using the strategies outlined in this book, you can share your feelings with your loved ones or close friends. These people can offer you the support needed when struggling with social phobia.

They can help you identify relapse signs and advise you what to do to manage anxiety and overcome relapse. Where else can you find help?

The best-placed people to help detect relapse signs are those who are close to us. These can be family members or friends. These people may help not only in detecting changes or signs of a relapse but also offer necessary support.

When feeling anxious, you can rely on loved ones to offer you support to overcome your fears. Having friends and loved ones can help you avoid negative thoughts and start thinking constructively.

Some people find it difficult sharing anxiety stories and their general experience with social phobia with loved ones because of various reasons. If you fall into this category, it would be advisable to join a group or an organization where you'll find it easy listening to other people's stories and sharing yours.

By joining help groups, a person struggling with social phobia will be able to meet people with the same condition and people who are ready to share part of their stories about the struggle with anxiety. Joining these groups helps a lot because, as an individual, you'll come out stronger after sharing your experience and learning anxiety management strategies used by others in managing social phobia.

Another option which we have already discussed in different chapters of this book is consulting a mental health specialist. Your mental health specialist will be able to assess and advise you on the best treatment options suitable for you. If a particular medication doesn't work for you, your doctor will be able to prescribe the right medication, depending on your situation.

In case your social phobia turns out being severe, your mental health specialist will also advise and give you the right information.

If a relapse occurs after following every social phobia treatment strategy, a person must learn how to reduce its intensity. By reducing the intensity of a relapse, a person manages to reduce the impacts this relapse can have on their life. As we saw earlier, after noticing that a relapse has occurred, it is important to identify factors that triggered it. This should then be followed by a prevention strategy to help avoid the same from happening in future.

If a relapse occurs, a person should avoid being discouraged and should, instead, learn how to collect the pieces and move on while focused on how to prevent another relapse in future.

A relapse is a very common thing, and you should never be disheartened if you experience one. The best thing to do is to stay focused on how to prevent it from happening again. Come up with a solid plan that can help you handle the effects of a relapse.

Learn everything relevant to your social phobia from symptoms through causes to effects on your life and available treatment options you can use to overcome it. Try to find time to interact with workmates or classmates in order to manage your anxiety and learn to understand your situation.

Avoidance of social situations in the name of being judged negatively or being humiliated should be history if at all you want to stop social phobia from denying you quality life. Do not allow what happened in the past to prevent you from reaching your full potential. Focusing on the past takes the precious time you would have spent on dealing with your current situation.

If you are trying to recover from social phobia, you should not expect results within a day or two. Treatment of social phobia is a process that can take weeks, months or even years. You should also understand that treatment guidelines and instructions should be followed as advised. This book has discussed the strategies that can be used in the treatment of social phobia, but it would be wise if you use what has been discussed here alongside what your mental health specialist recommends. If anything, you'll find that the same information covered in this book doesn't vary from what your doctor recommends.

Continue being optimistic as you embark on your journey to stop social phobia and maintain positive thinking all the way until you find the answer. Don't forget that you are not alone in this. There are several other people out there who have successfully defeated social phobia. You can also start enjoying your life by following the strategies discussed in this book.

Be a friend to yourself

Research indicates that many people struggling with social phobia also experience low self-esteem in life. These people constantly worry about themselves a lot. They always worry about what may happen if they fail to meet certain personal expectations.

As a person struggling with social phobia, it is important to not only get support from close friends and loved one but also encourage and support yourself. Encouragement and support that comes from you means more than any other support you could ever get from somewhere else. If you fail to do as you expected, do not condemn yourself or allow negative thoughts to get control over you.

Encouraging yourself despite failing on what you expected to do is a very important strategy for defeating anxiety and soldiering on toward victory. Don't forget that your fight against social phobia can take months or years. Expect to go through ups and downs as you try to conquer social phobia. It is a difficult and challenging fight that only you understand what it is.

Reward yourself after some time, especially after noticing improvements in your struggle with social phobia. Try to identify and recognize small goals that you have managed to achieve.

Managing social phobia is definitely going to take time. It would be right to consult your GP if you still encounter problems conquering anxiety.

FREEDOM
FROM
FEAR